It's me... a Cat

An imprint of Om Books International

First Published in 2019 by

Om KIDZ | Om Books International

Corporate & Editorial Office
A-12, Sector 64, Noida 201 301
Uttar Pradesh, India
Phone: +91 120 477 4100
Email: editorial@ombooks.com
Website: www.ombooksinternational.com

Sales Office
107, Ansari Road, Darya Ganj
New Delhi 110 002, India
Phone: +91 11 4000 9000
Email: sales@ombooks.com
Website: www.ombooks.com

ISBN: 978-93-86410-43-6

Printed in India

10 9 8 7 6 5 4 3 2 1

Contents

WHO ARE YOU?

Hello! I am a cat and I belong to the Felidae family. We are known for our grace, **inquisitiveness**, cleanliness and personality.

Scientific Name

Felis catus

A new word to learn

Inquisitive - showing an interest in learning

WHAT DO YOU LIKE TO EAT?

We are carnivores and we feed on rats, small birds and other rodents. We also love eating meat and fish.

No Milk, Please

You will be surprised to know that some cats are lactose intolerant. Consuming milk or milk products can cause vomiting and diarrhoea in cats.

WHAT ARE YOUR SPECIAL FEATURES?

I have a low-slung, supple body, a finely-moulded head, and a long tail which helps me maintain my balance. I have sharp teeth and claws which help me hunt for food.

Look at My Ears Move

We can rotate our ears up to 180 degrees and also pinpoint the source of the sound.

DO YOU HAVE A FLEXIBLE BODY?

Yes. Our bodies are very flexible because our spinal column is held together by muscles and not ligaments. We can easily contract, elongate and curve our bodies.

Digitigrade

Cats are digitigrade, which means they can walk on their toes.

WHERE DO YOU LIVE?

Cats can adapt to a variety of habitats and they are found across continents, except Antarctica. Feral cats can be found in grasslands, coastal areas, the tundra, forests, urban areas, agricultural lands, wetlands and scrublands.

Solitary vs Group Living

While cats are mostly solitary creatures, sometimes, they do live in groups.

WHO ALL ARE THERE IN YOUR FAMILY?

Our family, Felidae, has 37 species of cats that also include our wild relatives— cheetahs, lions, tigers, jaguars, pumas, leopards and lynx. While the larger cats such as lions and tigers, are ferocious and dangerous; indoor cats are friendly and playful.

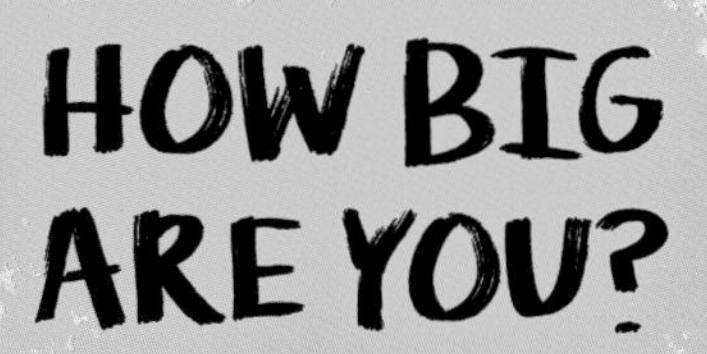

A household cat weighs between 3 to 5 kg; while non-pedigreed cats can weigh as much as 13 kg. Male cats are 28 inches long, while female cats are 20 inches long. We have a small gut and our small intestine is three times the length of our body.

Red British Male Cat

WHAT ARE YOUR BABIES CALLED?

My young ones are called kittens. Newborns are dependent on their mother. Kittens are born blind and deaf. They open their eyes almost 7 to 10 days after their birth and their ear canals open only after they are a week old.

Litter Size

We commonly have a litter size of three to five kittens.

Like Wild Cats

Just like my wild relatives, I am carnivorous, agile, powerful and well-coordinated in my movements.

HOW DO YOU COMMUNICATE?

We communicate by purring, growling, hissing and meowing. We also communicate through our scent. Our head-bumping behaviour is a way of depositing scents on substrates, including human beings.

Expressing Affection

Pet cats express their affection by rubbing their head, chin or tail against their owners .

WHAT IS YOUR LIFESPAN?

Usually, we have an average lifespan of around 3 to 5 years, when in the wild. Indoor cats, however, have been known to live up to 15 years or more. A cat's lifespan depends on the conditions it is exposed to.

Our Eyes Shine in the Dark

Our eyes are very sensitive to light due to the presence of a guanine layer, causing them to shine at night.

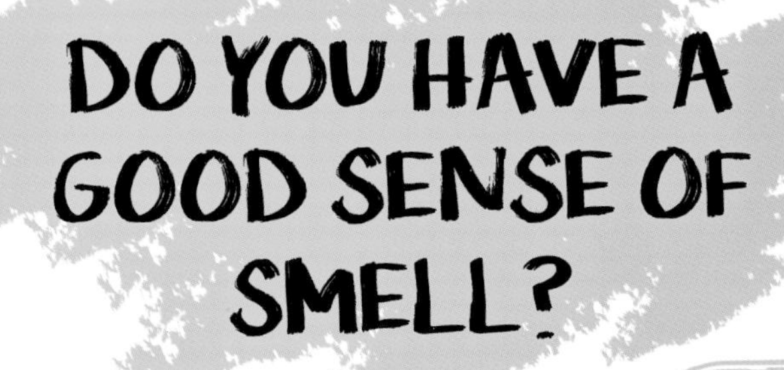

Yes, we have an excellent sense of smell and touch. Our sense of smell helps us to evaluate our food.

Landing on Our Feet

We are well coordinated and powerful. We are nimble-footed and if we fall, or are dropped from a height, we land up on our feet easily.

DO YOU HAVE TEETH?

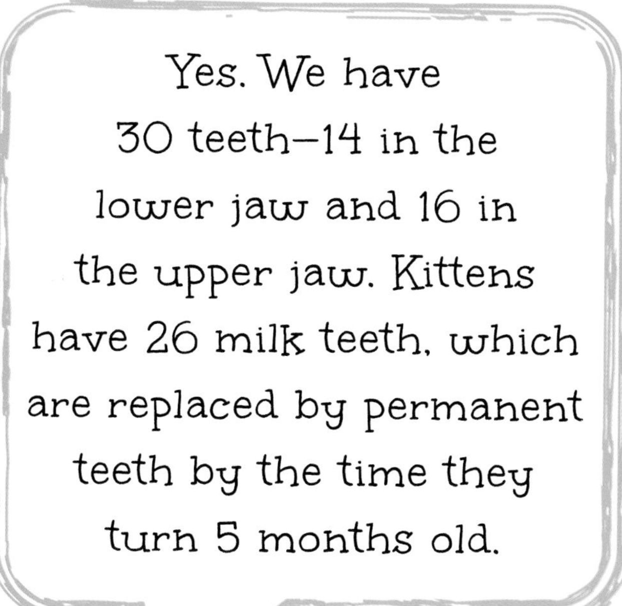

We Can't Chew Food

Since we do not have any flat-crowned teeth, we cannot chew our food.

DO YOU SLEEP?

Yes. We sleep for over 16 hours a day. However, our sleep patterns are very different from that of human beings. We are light sleepers, and have an episodic sleep pattern that helps us to be alert.

Conserving Energy

Sick cats go inactive. They withdraw themselves to conserve their energy. Cats rest to heal naturally.

WHO ARE SIAMESE CATS?

Exotic and Regal

Siamese cats appear very regal. They have **exotic** colours on their body, and are known to be loyal animals.

WHO ARE SPHYNX CATS?

Sphynx cats belong to the breed of hairless domestic cats. They need care and must be bathed regularly to ensure that their skin is free of oils. They have very large ears which require regular cleaning in order to get rid of the wax, dirt and dust that accumulate in them.

Energetic Bundles of Joy

Sphynx cats are known to be very friendly, energetic and playful pets.

WHO ARE PERSIAN CATS?

Persian cats belongs to the breed of long-haired cats. Known for our elegance, we have a shorter **muzzle** and a shorter tail, than the other species.

A new word to learn

Muzzle - Projecting part of the face

Intelligent Creatures

Persian cats are extremely intelligent and they enjoy being petted and pampered. They require daily grooming to keep their hair clean and hygienic.

WHY ARE CATS WORSHIPPED?

Egyptians domesticated cats because they realised the value of cats in protecting their granaries from rodents. Their adoration and respect for cats led to the formation of cat cults and temple worship.

The Cat Goddess

Egyptians were known to worship the Cat Goddess, Bastet, who was represented in the form of half, woman half feline.

WHAT SUPERSTITIONS ARE ASSOCIATED WITH CATS?

Black cats have been linked to a lot of superstitions and are believed to have occult powers. They are associated with black magic too!

Common Myths

Cats have been a part of the religions in Egypt, parts of Asia and the Nordic countries.

ACTIVITY TIME

FUN WITH ORIGAMI

Things You'll Need

- Origami paper
- Glue stick
- Marker
- Scissors

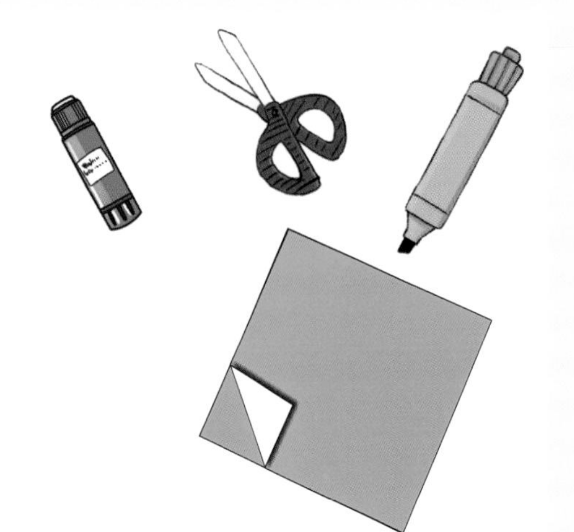

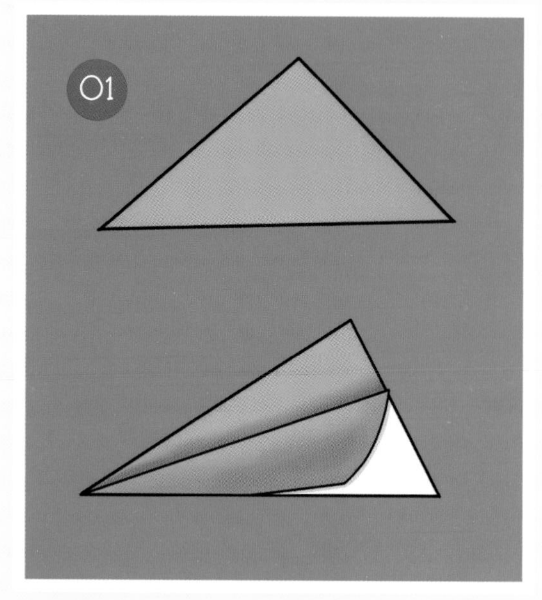

Fold the origami paper diagonally into half with the white side up. Fold the top corner of the triangle to meet the bottom edge.

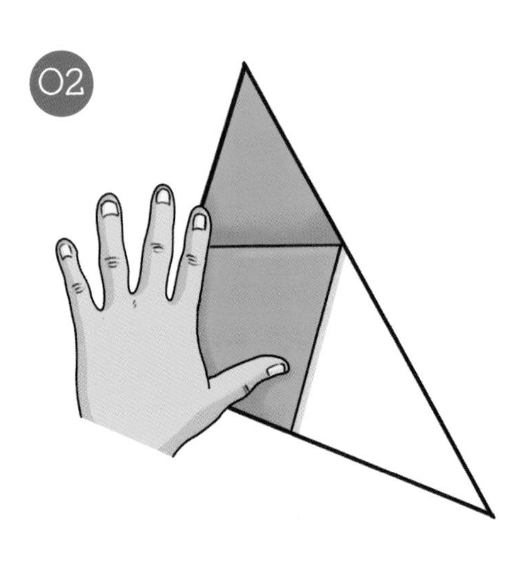

Fold the triangle into half in a manner that the left corner of the triangle meets the right corner.

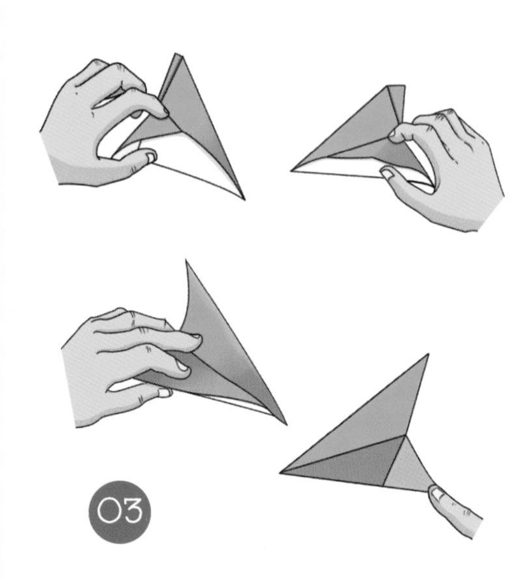

Pull the flap of the paper, so that the side meets the bottom edge of the triangle.

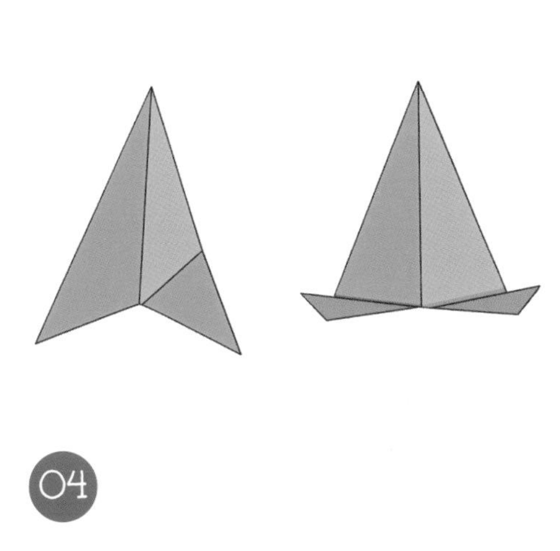

Rotate the paper and fold the two bottom corners upwards, to make the cat's body.

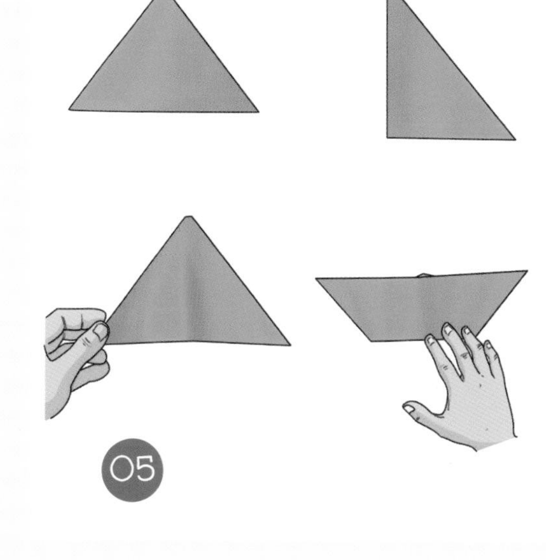

Take another paper and fold it diagonally into half, twice over. Open up the previous fold. Fold the top point of your triangle down to the bottom edge to make the cat's face. Fold the right corner of the triangle upward to meet the lower crease.

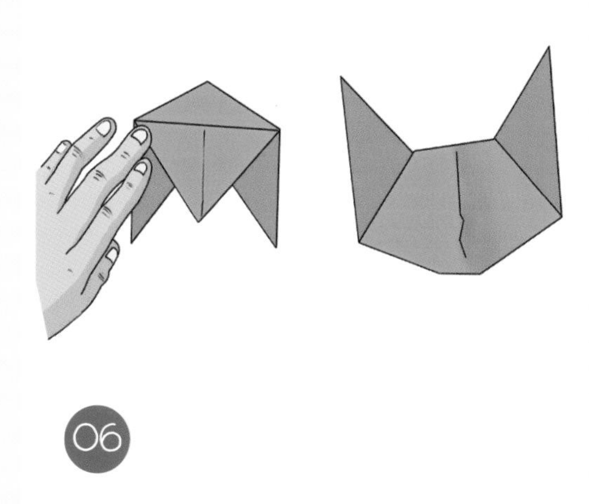

Place a finger inside the folded triangle. Now carefully push that top layer of the triangle down with one hand. With the other hand carefully push down the corner that's popping up. Rotate it. Then, fold the middle point underneath to create a cat face.

Paste the face and body together. Cut out a pair of eyes, and paste them on the face. Your cat is ready!

Help the cat find
its way to the mouse.